CU00868110

LITTLE WOMEN
INVEST

Preface by Paola Profeta

LAURA TARDINO

authorHOUSE®

AuthorHouse™ UK
1663 Liberty Drive
Bloomington, IN 47403 USA
www.authorhouse.co.uk
Phone: UK TFN: 0800 0148641 (Toll Free inside the UK)
UK Local: (02) 0369 56322 (+44 20 3695
6322 from outside the UK)

Published by AuthorHouse 08/24/2022

ISBN: 978-1-7283-7487-1 (sc)
ISBN: 978-1-7283-7486-4 (e)

Print information available on the last page.

This book is printed on acid-free paper.

CONTENTS

Preface by Paola Profeta ix

Introduction xiii

Chapter 1   Little Women Invest 1

Chapter 2   Marmee's advice.. 6

Chapter 3   Aunt March's lessons in Macro and
             Microeconomics 14

Chapter 4   Amy and Equities.................................... 22

Chapter 5   B as Beth and Bond 29

Chapter 6   M as Meg and materials........................... 34

Chapter 7   F as Family and Fund 41

Chapter 8   Jo, the future of finance 46

Chapter 9   Jo's friends.. 56

Conclusions and Acknowledgments 77

Little women invest
Laura Tardino
Little women Invest

"I'm not afraid of storms because
I'm learning to steer my boat."
L. M. Alcott

PREFACE
BY PAOLA PROFETA*

*Professor of Finance at Bocconi University and Director of Axa Gender Equality Lab.

They called it "Shecession", the female recession caused by the Covid19 pandemic. Women are more vulnerable than men on the labour market, already in the second quarter of 2020 there were 470 thousand less employed than in the same period of 2019 Today more than ever, in the face of the uncertainty of the future, female work is an essential resource: for women, for their economic independence which ensures against the work and family risks of families and for the entire country. Women's work means economic growth, enhancement of talents and human capital.

The current global pandemic crisis has highlighted the uncertainty and risks of the future. Women are more cautious and more risk averse than men: generations of my students know that, as Christine Lagarde said, if Lehman Brothers had been Lehman Sisters (or rather, Brothers and Sisters) the 2008 financial crisis would have perhaps had less catastrophic effects than we have experienced.

But women are also less prepared to manage money and savings, especially in South Europe. According to data from "Global Findex", in the possession of a current account the percentage of men exceeds that of women by 4.5%. This is not the case in other countries, such as Finland and Denmark, where the percentage of men and women with current accounts is the same, or like Sweden or Germany where women outnumber men. Again according to Global Findex, more than 60% of Italians who ask for a loan from financial institutions are men, while more than 70% of Italians who ask for a loan from family or friends are women. In other words, even today women still struggle to turn to financial institutions and encounter difficulties and obstacles in accessing credit. The consequences of this gap are not to be underestimated: fewer initial resources, less financial knowledge, less access to banks and financial instruments become a trap that relegates women to a subordinate role in financial decisions. Getting informed, getting to know, evaluating represent the way out. For this reason, our country established in 2017 the Committee for the planning and coordination of financial education activities, which promotes financial education and pays particular attention to girls. Today more than ever, this activity is essential: to cope with current and future uncertainties and make conscious life choices consistent with one's goals, it is necessary to learn how to manage one's savings, invest one's money, plan future.

About thirty years ago, we, two little women, Laura and Paola, met sitting in the front row in classroom 201 in via Sarfatti 25, on the first day of university. Friends immediately, united in the study, we have always "dreamed with ambition" as Kamala Harris, the first elected vice president of the United States, said on the day of her recent election. And we have grown confident in our energy, in our commitment, despite the ups and downs and difficulties, as in everyone's life.

What if that day thirty years ago we hadn't entered a classroom at Bocconi University? Would we have been able to manage our work and financial, insurance and social security choices in these years and those to come? Yet, these are important life choices for everyone and everyone ...

This book was born from a brilliant idea of my friend Laura and is aimed to all little women (but not only!) who have not studied and will not study economics, who live far from the world of finance, who have no specific knowledge in macroeconomics or mathematics, but who, following the simple lessons and advice of an expert in the field, can learn to invest in their future and in that of our country.

INTRODUCTION

Few pages, an handbook for young women who do not work in the financial sector but want to understand when we talk about spreads and Bund, S&P500, futures, stock exchanges and black swans on the news.

Many times, in recent years, I have in fact happened to answer the question "what work do you do?" and many times having given, I think, the simplest possible answer, I was told "I could never do it" or "I don't understand anything about it" or, worse, thinking that I worked for the tax office, I've seen people disappear. Trust me, it really happened!

More and more often in recent years, many young girls have asked me the question, now emancipated and economically independent, like Jo in the famous novel by Louisa May Alcott Little Women, feel even more the need to know this subject. It is a trend that will continue and for this reason I decided to write my first little book dedicated to them, combining a passion (mine, for writing) and the experience gained on the ground in twenty plus years of work in the world of investments after a business degree.

Simplicity of language, therefore, as a promise for these few pages which, supported by a good use of Google, I am sure will help you to better understand the world of investments.

Simplicity, also because, as Warren Buffet says: "Investing is simple, but it's not easy". The greatest risk is that of not knowing what we are doing, of losing control of our boat perhaps right in the middle of the storm, as also happened to the famous writer of Little Women who found herself several times, during her life, in financial difficulties but never gave up her independence and, investing in herself and her ability to write, without leaving the helm, earned the money that would have allowed her to maintain herself and her family.

If investing in ourselves by studying and working is the premise for our emancipation on which we have been working for some time thanks also to the messages and testimonies of many writers, investing our savings in the financial markets in a conscious and rational way is the next frontier to look to.

So what would Marmee and Aunt March say to the little women of the new millennium today? Pursuing passions to fulfill oneself professionally and personally is as important as thinking rationally about one's own economic wellbeing and, if once upon a time girls were advised to look for the best scion, today the logic of the good match could be at least reduced, giving more room for a good financial education.

1

LITTLE WOMEN INVEST

Louisa May Alcott wrote Little Women in 1868 and, many years later, that was my first novel. Jealously kept in the library of my bedroom, blue cardboard cover, dimensions not exactly pocket sized which made reading certainly uncomfortable given the nontrivial heaviness in my hands, lying under the blanket, blue as well.

Read and read many times and seen and seen at least as many at the cinema and on TV, I still appreciate its absolute modernity. A few years ago I saw at the cinema the last film based on the same, this time expertly directed by Greta Gerwig and I got the idea of writing a guide on the world of investments entitled more or less in the same way, to bring to young women several messages starting from the first: that the world is changing, or perhaps it has already partially changed, and women have been protagonists of this change and in my opinion they will continue to be so.

The novel, for those who have never read it or seen it at the cinema and I recommend you do it, revolves around the story of four sisters with whom it is almost impossible not to identify: the March sisters, different archetypes of young girls with a common denominator, the modest origins, and each with her own strengths and weaknesses.

There is Meg, the eldest, the most mature: sociable, sweet, maternal, she loves shopping and social life which, growing up, she will give up in the name of her family and three children. There is Jo (my favourite, and I don't think only mine), frank, courageous, restless but also tenacious, goodnatured and with a great passion and a great dream: to become a writer to be economically independent, refusing to accept the marriage of interest. There is Beth, sensitive and selfless, shy and shy, she hates being around people but loves music and the piano. Finally there is Amy, spoiled, vain, she loves art pursuing the dream of becoming a painter, she becomes a beautiful and refined woman, a lover of travel, the favourite of Aunt March, who will travel with her leaving the States United and crossing Europe.

Each of them embodies timeless dreams and desires such as beautiful clothes, worldly life, economic and social wealth, art and music and the desire to chase them, chase them and grab them, in a historic moment certainly not easy for the "weaker sex". The shrewish Aunt March doesn't use half words, leaves no room for misunderstanding when she reminds her nieces that only a good marriage can make them rich and happy. In those years, marriage was the only "safe" way, if well thought out. A woman had no choice, unless she was already rich. According to Aunt March, the only alternative to marriage was the brothel or the stage which were often, according to her, synonyms. But nevertheless the niece Jo decides, at least in the first of Alcott's novels, not to give in to marriage and good luck, managing to finish her manuscript, to sell it and to help her family with the money he earned.

I believe that even Aunt March would change her mind about marriage if she had the chance to take a journey through time to the present day and that Jo, without hesitation, would be proud to have brought forward a cause as modern as it is revolutionary in times really not suspicious. Alcott's novel is a manifesto of positive feminism, the one that springs from the awareness of being different from men and different from each other but that, however we think it and that whatever profession we aspire to, commitment, determination, constancy are fundamental to achieve economic independence (even more than a good match!) and today, fortunately, few of us have an aunt March next to us to be convinced of all this.

Indeed, I think that today Aunt March could give different lessons because the world has really changed. And that, on the other hand, there are many more Marmee, the mother of the four little women, and Louis Alcott, famous for the phrase "better a happy spinster than an unhappy wife or silly young lady running around looking for a husband".

If determined and ambitious like Jo, many women today have the opportunity not only to study and find a job but to make a career and, even if disparities in terms of success and salary remain with respect to men, they can finally be economically independent, help family management, spend and save. We no longer need a good match as the main road for our economic independence, we are freer in our sentimental choices and, finally, we not only earn but spend and save.

With my book I would like to project the female world even further. Beyond savings, in the world of investments. **To be able to invest, in fact, you need to have some savings I would not recommend borrowing money to do so** and that is why, for centuries, the world of investments has been a world of only men and continues in some ways to be dominated by them. In the past, it was mainly men who had the money to invest and they mainly turned to other men as the world of work was dominated by them.

Today, however, women have growing savings to invest and, in recent decades, the percentage of women working in the financial sector has definitely increased, just as, albeit much more slowly, the number of women who matter is increasing, managers, so to speak, who make important investment decisions and / or direct entire teams dedicated to this or that functional area, in any case, to the management of other people's money.

Companies, banks, investors cannot think of remaining immobile spectators in front of this pink revolution. Pink money will constitute a growing part of the money in circulation and will be increasingly spent on "pink goods and services" just as "pink savings" will constitute a gradually increasing share of the overall savings to be invested.

Modern Little women must acquire more financial awareness and be ready to exploit it by becoming good managers of themselves and their savings, even if they have not studied economics and finance at university. I don't do fashion to write little women in suits and give tips on how to dress during a job interview or daybyday at the office. I have been a portfolio manager, investment strategist and, finally, sales for some European asset management companies. Many of these words are still unclear today to many girls who during a lesson, it doesn't matter if during pilates, wellness or yoga, or waiting at the beautician, the hairdresser or at the supermarket checkout, they ask me what I do.

I decided to write Little Women Invest, borrowing the characters of Alcott's novel, to bring my world to them with simplicity, a bit of what some call *financial education*, or the knowledge of a few and simple elements that will allow, I hope, many more young women to juggle in the future between banks, consultants, online platforms when they invest their savings because, as Warren Buffet says, still he, the real risk arises from not know what we are doing.

2

MARMEE'S ADVICE

I would like Mrs. March, Marmee, the most important reference figure for the four little women invested with the dual role of mother and head of the family as her husband left for the war, to give some practical advice to initiate the little women to the world of finance as a mother would do.

Marmee is in fact pragmatic wise and only thanks to her the four sisters will be able in the novel to face the difficulties of life, treasuring the precepts received from an early age. Marmee is at the same time sweet and generous but endowed with a very strong temperament, capable not only of raising her four daughters alone and penniless, but of educating them according to modern canons. "I am angry almost every day of my life" she says to her daughter Jo, denouncing her opposition to the way in which women are treated and educated in those years. Marmee is for the emancipated woman, economically independent, capable of managing her finances in order to cope with the inclement weather of life, as indeed happens to her in the pages of the book.

I am sure that, if you could relive today between the lines of this manuscript, she would begin by saying that investing our savings is an extremely serious activity, on which depends what will be the ability of everyone to meet the economic needs they will have in the course of life, of which we ignore unexpected events and probabilities and, above all, the duration.

We do not know how many years we will live or how we will live them and therefore we may more or less need the money set aside once we have stopped working, but we do not even know what will happen to us before we retire. A marriage, even the most informal, the birth of one or more children, their growth, a trip or the purchase of an house, etc. etc., they require a lot of money. Not to mention all the expenses after retirement! Often, to meet these expenses, the salary is not enough or is not anymore an option and it is necessary to draw from the savings that, if appropriately invested, during the course of a working life, can make a significant contribution.

And even if all this seems very far in time, **it is good to start thinking about it from an early age because small amounts saved and invested every month for a life can really do the difference when we retire**.

Better to be prepared as we do with maths and English and invest small amount of the first salaries destined for savings as soon as possible.

Furthermore, although it may seem strange, **we should think about savings and therefore about investments even before spending**, at least for the superfluous ones, leaving the remaining money to the latter. Very often, especially as young people, we first think about meeting the expenses (not just those, let's say, strictly necessary) and then we think about a possible saving and only finally about how to invest it.

I read in a specialized magazine that only 37% of Italian women, or one in 3, invest their savings (compared to 48% of men) even though 67% of women save. We save but we don't invest. We are farsighted, that is, we look at future uncertainties with responsibility, but we do not have the habit of doing it in a more "scientific" way, that is, with the correct tools. And it is above women who do not work and those who are not familiar with these tools, because they have not studied economics and finance, to look with suspicion at investments.

On the contrary everyone can learn, and even in a short time, in order to change these statistics so that more and more women can invest their savings increasing their personal wellbeing as well as the social one because in the future everyone of us will be able to count less and less on the so called state welfare, or in other terms the classic grandmother's pension.

Knowing what to invest in and how, what to expect from your investments and in how much time, is very important as studying English and maths because it removes the fear of the unknown on the one hand and on the other it helps in the dialogue with who helps us plan our investments.

Yes, because Marmee's advice would be **do not do by yourself** and to pay close attention to the **risk** involved. I have known many people who, by approaching investments in financial markets such as a game table or a roulette wheel, have lost their life savings. Any investment is associated with an uncertain **gain** which is not known a priori. When we buy the shares of a company or bonds of a state, we know the purchase price but not their future price. This may be higher or lower and will continuously change over time. There is therefore a risk that my investment will lead me to suffer a **loss**.

To avoid unpleasant surprises or, what is worse, to find ourself without money in times of need, it is advisable to ask for help from an expert if you do not have a thorough knowledge of the markets and / or the opportunity to monitor their progress constantly and regularly.

Neither more nor less than a doctor.

The finance doctor is usually found virtually in a platform or physically in a bank and is called **financial consultant**: it is him who directs us, consulting in turn a series of extremely numerous financially educated professionals that help him understand what is the best "solution" for us.

In fact, when we are sick, we go to the doctor, who after a careful visit to better understand who we are, if we have other pathologies and to avoid the presence of allergies, will diagnose us and prescribe a treatment. The cure can require one or more medicines, a correct diet, physical activity which, together, will allow us to heal.

The consultant, like the doctor, proposes an investment solution in which he can combine several financial instruments after, of course, listening to us carefully to get to know us and to understand our expectations in order to evaluate our risk appetite, that is our ability to bear any losses which depends on many factors.

The most important factor, when it comes to investments, is certainly the **time** which means not only for how many months we want to keep our savings locked in any financial instrument instead of our current account, ready to be spent, but even our age, because, depending on the moment we are living in, we will need more or less money to spend and the two things are therefore absolutely connected.

Just as a doctor would never prescribe certain medicines to a baby or child under the age of twelve, so a good financial advisor must absolutely take into consideration our age and our financial needs before "prescribing" any investment solution.

The university, the purchase of a house, the birth of a child are moments as beautiful in our life as they are expensive. Probably, in those moments, our savings could be particularly low compared to other moments but it is also true that, in front of us, in those periods we have many more years than we will have when we have finished university, or when our children have grown up and we have finished to buy an house.

In fact, **different financial instruments need different times to give their results**: just like medicines which, depending on the active ingredient, can take more or less time to heal the patient. **By and large, equity investments require more patience than some bond** investments, and we'll soon find out why.

In addition, **some investments can be sold and purchased daily**, while for others the purchase and sale can take weeks or months. Normally, the former are defined as **liquid** (the shares and many of the bonds are liquid) while the latter are called illiquid (a famous case of illiquid is certainly investment in real estate, or houses). **An illiquid investment can take up to several months before it can be sold** to make cash in case of need and, if we don't have liquid investments, we can sell quickly in a few days, this could put us in troubles.

In the following pages we will talk about liquid investments because they constitute an universe in themselves already very extensive and interesting to start with.

Investing is therefore a function of time because different financial investments require different times to make a profit. This is why we speak of a **time horizon**, to indicate the time that we are willing to grant to our investment so that it generates its potential gain.

It is important to know, however, that the risk of incurring in a loss is never eliminated, but, with the right temporal evaluation it can decrease.

If we are young and we still have many years to live, our time horizon could be longer than that of a worker close to retirement who will soon no longer have a salary and will be forced to use his own savings. If we don't like the idea of blocking our savings for a long time, our time horizon may be shorter than that of a less worried friend even if older.

A good financial advisor builds the most suitable investment solution for his client starting from his time horizon and his **risk appetite, i.e how much we are willing to lose**. Both depend on many factors, both objective (age, personal wealth, family unit, etc. etc.) and subjective (personal attitude, character, emotionality, etc. etc.). For this, the consultant must know us and propose the solution that best suits us. We will therefore have to tell our consultant everything (or almost everything), just like the sisters with Marmee or a patient with a doctor.

The consultant cannot know in advance when and how much the gain from the investment suggested by him will materialize and he knows that there is a risk of loss. The evolution of the price of an investment is subject to multiple factors (macroeconomic and microeconomic scenario, valuations, exogenous shocks I will describe later on) all beyond the control of the financial advisor.

For this reason, a good investment solution is made up of multiple instruments and follows the principle of the **diversification**, in order to reduce the weight that the single instrument has on the entire investment in case something goes wrong. Having the shares of a single company can be very risky if that company goes bankrupt one day. Better then to have a set of shares of different companies to risk less. The principle of diversification is very important when we decide to invest our money because it allows us to reduce the risk of significant losses. Diversifying means considering more instruments and better if these instruments have a different trend, ie their price does not rise or fall at the same time for the same cause. **In other words a well diversified portfolio is made up of several decorrelated financial instruments**.

The financial instruments at our disposal are generally speaking **stocks, bonds, currencies and commodities**.

Even when we decide to buy a **pension fund or an insurance policy within it we will find stocks, bonds, currencies, commodities so it is good to know what they are**.

The March sisters will accompany us page after page in the attempt to understand them better but only after a modern aunt March will reveal what those instruments are for, what lies behind them, why they generate losses or gains of money, just like in the novel she drives the nieces to the right choice of the man to marry in order to settle down, thus investing in a good marriage. Certainly a different investment, but just as complex and not without risks as the financial one.

When we invest our money in stocks, bonds, currencies or other, it means that for a more or less prolonged period of time we are giving it to "someone" who, after that period of time, will give us back more or less money. This someone will use the money in the meantime to do something, but what? And who is to receive our money?

3

AUNT MARCH'S LESSONS IN MACRO AND MICROECONOMICS

Aunt March, the rich great aunt of the four sisters of the novel, a shrewish and lonely woman, very different in setting from Marmee, represents reason, measure, economic interest, as well as the spirit of her time. If Marmee, modern, puts sentiments and passion before money, without underestimating its value as well as the importance to believe in ourselves and realize our dreams and at the same timeto reach an economic independence, Aunt March overturns this perspective, giving life lessons to little women so that they can live up to the most classic of weddings for interest, knowing full well that, once the chicken is married, they will be able to do whatever they want. It is famous her sentence: "Nobody makes their way alone, least of all a woman". Aunt March is shrewd, calculating, cold but also generous and will decide at different times to remove and put on her will the name of one or more sisters, aware that her savings and everything she owns must be entrusted in a manner intelligent so that their value can continue to grow over time, even when she is gone.

Today, after 150 years, Aunt March could advise young modern women **how to choose a financial consultant**, less demanding from a sentimental point of view but certainly no less important from an economic point of view than an husband.

If it is nowadays possible to choose also by gender, because there are so many women financial advisors, it is nevertheless more important to choose a **professional**, serious and prepared who does not run away with our money and who decides to invest it well. Aunt March would tell us to be wary of the makeshift consultant who doesn't have a good resume on his shoulders, who doesn't work for a well recognized bank that can somehow guarantee us like the high sounding surname of a good wedding party.

But that's not enough!

Aunt March would for sure go further and teach to the young girls **some lessons of macro and microeconomics to be ready for the conversation with the financial consultant**.

Who receive the money we invest through the consultant? How is it used and why it can increase/ decrease over time? It could be useful to prepare ourselves to avoid being enchanted by the words of those who, instead of helping us in planning our investments taking into account our time horizon and our risk aversion, could make us losing all or part of our savings by choosing to give them to the wrong person/institution or at the wrong time or both.

Simplifying: our savings, if invested, in most cases will end up in the hands of a **State (macro)** and / or in the hands of a **Company (micro)** which will use the money received to build, in the first case, schools, hospitals, roads, to pay public employees etc. etc. e and, in the second case, to buy a new machinery or another company etc. etc.

It is therefore important to understand if that State or that Company are **solid** enough to be able to **return** the money lent and "something more", which we will see can take different forms depending on the case.

The proper functioning of each State and of every company can be controlled **monitoring key data** that are published every day on specific sites and commented on by economists, analysts, journalists, etc. etc.

In the case of states, these data are called macroeconomic data because they concern the economy as a whole, made up of all citizens, whether they are consumers, workers or entrepreneurs; in the case of individual companies, on the other hand, the data are called microeconomic. It is simple because macro and micro, intuitively, lead to think big (State) and small (single company).

The financial solidity of a state is measured by the growth of what it produces (it is called gross domestic product, GDP, and it is a number that expresses the sum of consumption, investments, exports net of imports and public expenditure or that made by the state) but also of inflation (i.e. the growth of prices), debt (money borrowed), unemployment rate. A solid state has a high

GDP and low level of debt and unemployment while inflation is under control, let's say around 2%. Troubled states from a financial point of view, on the other hand, have low growth, a lot of debt, many unemployed and out of control inflation (whether too high or too low).

Growth and debt, both in the public and in the private sector, depend also on the actions of the Government that, through **fiscal policy, decides how many and what taxes introduce** on companies (those to which the consultant will give your money) and on private citizens. More taxes therefore potentially mean less money for companies and private citizens but mean more money for the State and therefore potentially less public debt but greater growth if the money collected will be used well because the State will reinvest that money in new activities giving back that money to companies and private citizens in a complex net of interconnections.

Central Banks, on the other hand, move **monetary policy through the so called official interest rate**. Their role is very complex, in reality, as they have multiple responsibilities, the most immediate and important is perhaps the creation of money in circulation but it is above all in terms of inflation and economic growth that they have a considerable weight on our investments by manipulating interest rates.

The interest rate is the price of the currency left on deposit in a checking account. The higher this price, the more it costs to borrow money and the more difficult it becomes to get money to companies through banks. A higher interest rate is unpleasant for everyone because both corporations, states, and individuals will pay higher interest on debt incurred and may even decide not to borrow any more money. Conversely, a low interest rate facilitates loans to both companies and individuals. More loans mean more money in circulation. When Central Banks raise rates, we therefore speak of a restrictive policy (the quantity of money in circulation is reduced); otherwise, for an expansive policy. In the first case Central Banks behave as hawks and are defined hawkish while in the second they act as doves and their mood is defined dovish.

But why are these policies so important for savings and investments?

Money in circulation has two effects: one on inflation and the other on growth. So extremely simplified, if we have more money available (because loans are cheaper) we can also spend more asking for more goods (houses, cars, clothes, furniture, food) or services (gyms, spas, beauticians) and therefore contributing to the growth of the economy as a whole and also to the increase in prices because these depend precisely on demand (the higher it is, the more they rise and vice versa being the offer equal).

Of course, the opposite is true when the money in circulation decreases. Less demand for goods and services, less growth and less inflation.

Therefore central banks, by raising and lowering the official interest rate, can affect two fundamental variables such as the growth and inflation of an economy.

In fact, many other interest rates depend on the official interest rate, including those on mortgages for the purchase of houses, on loans granted by banks to households and businesses and the remuneration of the deposits of businesses and households in banks as well as government bond yields.

However, the official interest rate is not the only instrument available to Central Banks. Central Banks can intervene with more "invasive" instruments, using for example the Quantitative Easing or, in extremis, the so called Helicopter Money.

Quantitative Easing (monetary easing or, more simply, QE) means the purchase of government bonds (these are the bonds we will discuss later) by the Central Bank with the currency it has created, while by Monetary Helicopter we mean the direct distribution of the money created to the citizens. The money put into circulation aims to increase once again, as in the case of lower interest rate, consumption and investments.

Each state or confederation of states has its own Central Bank: in Europe it is the European Central Bank (ECB) that prints the euro and directs the monetary policy for all countries of the Monetary Union.

The ECB was founded in 1998 and is today under the leadership of a woman for the first time since its creation: Christine Lagarde.

The ECB always communicates its decisions on Thursdays, usually the first of the month.

In the United States, the central bank is called the Federal Reserve (FED) and was created in 1913. Economists, analysts and investors await its rate decisions once every two months according to a specific calendar.

In the UK, the Bank Of England (BOE) was created in 1694 but only after 1844 it became a national institution and a model for all the other, younger, Central Banks.

Any investor cannot ignore the activities of these three main central banks, just as it is advisable to monitor the macroeconomic and microeconomic data that many organizations (IMF, OECD, Worl Bank, etc etc) publish on a daily basis. These are numbers relating to a given period for which an estimate is normally drawn up (the so called expected value).

Among the main macroeconomic data: the growth of the gross domestic product, unemployment, inflation, the debt / GDP ratio and the deficit / GDP ratio. The deficit measures the difference between income and expenditure of the state during the year while the debt is equivalent to the accumulation of past deficits and all the interest to be paid on loans made to the state by bond investors.

Among the microeconomic data, the most important are the profits that all companies listed on the stock exchanges, or those that a financial advisor could tell you about, communicate to the public every three months and for this reason are called quarterly.

In the first weeks of January, April, July, October, every day dozens and dozens of listed companies announce to the world how their business has gone in the past quarter and give an idea of how it will go in the coming months.

The publication of these numbers is called the reporting season and four times a year fills the pages of any financial newspaper, drawing the attention of all financial operators.

The macro data and the micro data are so many that as there is no way to get bored because something recurring is communicated every day, not to mention that suddenly unexpected rumors and news can arrive, as gossips so much loved by Aunt March, and for their possible positive or negative impact on the global economy or on a single country, sector or company they could lead to buying or selling, contributing to create a fluctuation (volatility) in the value of investments.

4

AMY AND EQUITIES

The shares represent a portion of the capital of the company that issued them and are traded (listed) on regulated markets. When we buy one or more shares we somehow become "owners" of a more or less small portion of the company that issued them and we therefore share the good and bad luck of that company. The share price moves following the law of supply and demand. If the first exceeds the second it goes up, vice versa it goes down. In general, if the company is doing well (higher sales, lower production costs, etc.), the share price will reflect this trend going up because more people will be interested in having shares. Viceversa if the company will go badly the price will go down, downd till zero if the company should go bankrupt in extremis. Whoever buys a share is entitled to the so called annual dividend or a sum of money that the company recognizes to the shareholder as a share of the profits it created during the year. For this reason, when we buy a stock, the overall gain (yield) must take into account not only the change in the price but also the dividend received. If the price goes up, we earn; if the price goes down, we lose. In both situations the dividend will be an extra gain which, in the first case, is added to that deriving from the price while, in the second case, it will act as a buffer to the loss.

Normally, for the share price to reflect the company's ability to do business, we need to have some patience and that is why it is preferable to buy shares especially when we are young, like Amy, the youngest of the March sisters. In fact, we may have bought the shares in a time of macroeconomic crisis whereby the company, despite being successful in its sector, is experiencing a moment of decline in sales because consumers are buying less of what the company produces. If it is possible to wait without rushing to sell, that moment will pass and the share price of a successful company will rise again.

In general, all countries have a stock market, the so called stock exchange, where the shares of all publicly traded companies in that country are bought and sold. In America, the three main local indices are the S&P500, the DOWJONES and the NASDAQ, the latter made up of more than 2,500 stocks from technology related companies.

To facilitate every analysis, it could be of help to group companies by sector to which they belong (financial, industrial, public utility, pharmaceuticals, consumption, chemical, energy, technology, cyclical consumption, telecommunications, real estate) and several indices are used to compare their performance. If our advisor suggests us to buy Coca Cola shares, we can not only see how their price will go by following the daily changes, but we can also compare it versus the trend of the sector using the consumption index or more general versus the broader local index of the United States or even broader the world stock index. The most common sectoral or geographic indices are those created by Morgan Stanley, a famous American bank, and called MSCI.

When I started working in this sector, after a brief interlude spent behind the scenes in a risk analysis office, I was dealing with stocks: I was buying and selling stocks. It is a complex job because it requires the analysis of the balance sheets and income statements of companies and the day to day monitoring of economic news which, in some cases, could change your mind about the investment. There is no joking with shares because their price can vary significantly in a short time (it is said that it is volatile) and if you are not patient it is better to avoid them. An equity investment makes more sense if we have a long time horizon so that only in this way can we reduce the probability of incurring losses. We will see better shortly.

The "traders" are on the opposite people, sometimes well described by movies, attached to the monitors of a PC infront of the change of equities prices in real time who buy and sell the same shares within few hours or few days, giving up to the dividend and looking only at the price. It is not the approach that I would suggest to those who do not do this for a job.

It is not even the approach followed by Warren Buffet, a professional in the sector but with a completely different investment philosophy, the one I would like to suggest to everybody. Today in his nineties, Buffet is one of the richest men in the world and, just think, he started investing in stocks at the age of 11 using the money he earned by selling the drinks he bought in his grandfather's shop at school. Buffet buys stocks whose price is low and holds them for very long periods before selling at an higher price, when the stock becomes expensive.

It could be helpful to look at the history of the price using a graph going back to the past the longest possible, and understand if, compared to the past, the stock is expensive or not (technical analysis). To do this, the so called "multiples" are also used, ie how many times the current price reflects the expected turnover, profits or dividends (fundamental analysis). One of the most used indicator is the "price to earnings". But be careful to consider the right profits. Financial analysts, or those who express a purchase/sale judgment, often take into account the expected profits that will not necessarily be actually realized. For this reason, evaluations are extremely subjective and are not enough alone to assess a good investment in stock.

It is possible to calculate the multiples of each company, but also those of the sector or the country it belongs to using for example the multiples of MSCI indices by sectors and countries.

Multiples and graphs are the basis of the financial analyst's work. His judgment clearly depends on absolutely discretionary hypotheses and may therefore be different from the judgment of another analyst. For this reason it is always better to hear more voices and rework them before investing.

In the short term, buying a stock after months and months of price increases can expose to greater risks, because in the face of the slightest negative news, general or more specific, many will try to sell what they had bought. Conversely, when everyone has sold the low price could be convenient and it could be the right time to invest because, if you have enough patience, that price will sooner or later start to rise again. This attitude is called contrarian and in practice suggests going against the tide when violent corrections occur in the price of a stock or a stock index.

Finding the right time or the right price is by no means trivial and few succeed, even adopting a longer horizon, experience can help but the risk of incurring losses before eventually making a profit remains high, above all if we decide to "bet" on a single stock. Better then to diversify by choosing more companies or investments other than equities whose performances are decorrelated meaning that in face of unexpected bad news have a different reaction in terms of price.

Look at how American industrial stocks of the Dow Jones have performed from the early 1900s to the present! It is one of the longest time series we have.

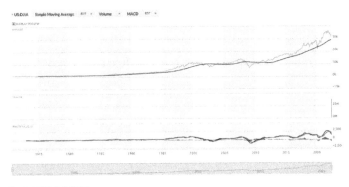

DOWJONES

At first glance it seems that the Dow Jones has always gone up. However, looking carefully at the graph, in many more or less prolonged moments, the index has dropped and sometimes even quite a lot. It happened for example in the late twenties, early seventies or in the early and late 2000s.

The corrections the stock indices, if very large this is the name of the reversals that lead to a significant decline, i.e. around 10% daily or more, coincide with the occurrence of negative events called *black swans* to indicate the low probability (all the swans are white) and therefore the absolute exceptionality of the same. The black swan theory, in fact, wants certain events to have much more impact on the markets than events considered normal.

Stock markets don't like black swans because they lead to violent corrections or the loss of value of stocks. If we have invested in stocks, the appearance of a black swan must cause us to worry because we could lose a good part of our savings in the short term. Conversely, if we haven't invested yet, the black swan can create good market conditions to start doing so. In any case, to sell is not a good option in the long run if we have not done before.

The great economic crisis of 1929 called the Great Depression, the oil shock of the early 1970s, the Asian Tiger crisis in the late 1990s, the bursting of the technology bubble in the early 2000s, the Great Financial Crisis (GCF) of 2008, the end of 2018 and, coming to our days, the Corona Virus which we will talk about later for its relevance, all represent examples of black swans.

In general, what happens when a black swan appears is that financial operators panic by not knowing what the economic consequences will be on the profits of companies and on the global economic growth, and run to sell the shares, fearing that their price will drop considerably.

It happened in 2001, 2008, 2018, 2020! It is not uncommon and can very negatively affect the performance of an investment especially if you have the misfortune to invest just before when the correction begins because, before starting to earn, it will be necessary to recover the heavy losses and this could require months, sometimes years.

The good news, as history shows, is that after a while it is very likely that the market recovers and in the long term the trend is up giving really a good opportunity of return.

5

B AS BETH AND BOND

When talking of something decorrelated with equities, with a different behaviour in terms of price reaction to news flow or suited for a shorter temporal horizon, as happens to the unfortunate Beth in the novel who will die prematurely from health problems, the first thought goes to bonds, in particular to bonds issued by governments.

It is therefore important to understand what bonds are (there are not only government bonds) and why they could behave differently from equities within a portfolio.

First, unlike equities, bonds are a loan that the investor makes to a State or a company and which gives the right at maturity to the repayment of the capital plus an interest on it, called coupon or yield, that is paid regularly once or twice the year. For this reason they are a less risky financial instrument than equities because whatever the evolution of the price of the bond will be in the holding period, it will return to 100 at maturity. If the price goes up the investment is increasing in capital terms, if it goes down it is loosing capital. But, at maturity, the price will always be

100, unless the government or the issuing company defaults due to the emergence of serious economic difficulties. It doesn't happen frequently for states but it can happen more frequently for corporates. If this happens, both the coupon and the bond price at maturity may be subject to a cut (the latter called hair cut) and the issuer will return less than the loaned capital to the creditor. In any case, the State and or the company at maturity are obliged to reimburse totally or partially the investor, an obligation that makes the investment less risky than the one in equity because, if the company fails the price of its equity will be zero.

During the investment period, the bond distributes to the investor normal interest annually or semi annually, in the form of a coupon, which helps to increase the profit or reduce the loss. Coupons are paid during the entire period between the time of purchase and maturity (the duration of the loan) and this also makes bond investment less risky than equities.

Each bond is characterized by a price, an yield, a duration and a rating on the degree of reliability of the issuer which gives an idea of its financial solidity, or its ability to return the money lent to the investor. The most solid companies are generally those with less debt while the most indebted ones are riskier and with higher coupons, which is why they are also called "high yield" or HY to distinguish them from the others (Investment Grade).

The rating is provided by companies called rating agencies.

The main ones are American: Moody's, Standard & Poor and Fitch, also called the three sisters. Their opinions, expressed in letters are well monitored by all the professional investors even if they are often published too late, while markets, as we have already mentioned in the previous pages, react ahead of news. Agencies tend to lower or raise their judgment when the macro or the micro picture has already worsened: the price of the bond may already have discounted the bad or good news before their announcement. However, there is always the possibility that agencies surprise investors with unexpected "moves".

In general, a higher yield corresponds to a higher risk because, to convince an investor to lend his money to a riskier state and or company, it is necessary to pay more interest on the loan itself, otherwise the investor will not do it.

For government or corporate bonds, as well as for equities, there are indices that group them by country, sector or rating. The most famous are those developed by the well-known American bank JP Morgan. An index is a number that expresses the average price of a group of bonds or their average yield. The indices allow you to compare a bond to a group of bonds to understand how its price or yield is moving in relative terms. The spread indicates the difference in yield between two bonds or between two bond indices or between a bond and an index. Italian bonds, called BTPs, are often compared with those issued by Germany (called Bunds). To say that the 10year Italian BTP has a spread of 1% over Germany means that it yields 1% more than the 10year Bund: if the yield on the Bund is 1%, the BTP yields 2%.

The spread became famous in Italy (and in the so called PIIGS countries, ie Portugal, Ireland Greece and Spain other than Italy) few years ago during the "European sovereign crisis" of 2010. Since then, newspapers and television news have never lost sight of it and, whenever it rises, they come out with headlines that warn of what's happening.

The spread indicates, in fact, how much one bond yields more than another, thus measuring its riskiness because higher yields correspond to higher risks. Each time the spread between BTPs or Bonos and Bunds rises, it means that Italian/Spanish bonds yield more than German bonds, but this happens because investors have sold the BTPs and Bonos, fearful of the risk associated with Italy or Spain and their price will go down while the yield will, in fact, go up. This is not liked by investors who already have bought BTPs or Bonos (as the price has dropped), nor to the Italian and the Spanish Government, which will have to pay more interest (the yield goes up) on the money borrowed through the issue of government bonds.

I know, it is not immediate but two are the main relationships to keep in mind for bonds: 1. risk goes up/yield goes up; 2 the yield goes up/ the price goes down. When the price of a bond is low and therefore attractive, it becomes crucial to understand if that bond is really risky and likely to default, or if the seller's reaction has been exaggerated and the state/company that issued it will actually be able to meet its commitment by maturity. In one case or another, it is important to analyse well the debt and the cash available both at the private level for the individual company and at the public level for the individual state.

The following graph describes the trend in the yield of the US Treasury at 10 years, i.e. the bond issued by the American Government with a duration of 10 years. USA, for various reasons, are considered an economically sound country and therefore low risk, its rating has always been very high (AAA or triple A tht means maximum macroeconomic security) for this reason it is also said than the return associated with this security is the risk free return.

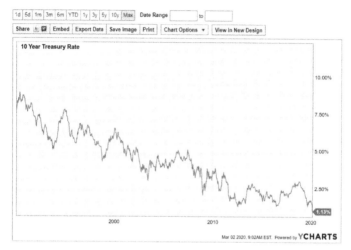

10Y TREASURY

Over the last thirty years, the yield on American bonds with a ten year duration has gradually fallen from over 8% to 1.13%! This means that if we buy a 10year US bond, we are lending your money to the US state for the next ten years at an annual rate of 1.13%. This is what happened also to the Bund and to the BTP as a result of the QE of the FED and the ECB: i.e. the purchase of central bank securities has caused the price to rise and the yield to fall. In this period the price of the bond may go up or down but in 10 years it will be equal to today's issue price, or 100. We could also decide not to buy at the issuance and to sell before the maturity, in this cases the price difference will change the overall return.

6

M AS MEG AND MATERIALS

Equities and bonds are undoubtedly the most common financial instruments. A good financial advisor is someone who proposes a portfolio made up of a "right" combination of equities and bonds, which takes into account the time horizon, risk aversion, and the economic needs of his client.

However, it is possible to complete the portfolio by buying the so called commodities (not only oil and gold, which I am sure you have heard about, but also sugar, orange juice, palladium, pork belly ...) and currencies (dollar, yen, pound, but also the most exotic).

In general, these are very liquid investments and are bought and sold night and day. For this reason, they turn out to be extremely volatile and therefore risky (i.e. their price moves really fast, even during the day), much more than equities.

Investments for wealthy people like the ambitious and snobbish Meg?

Perhaps yes, due to the risks they expose to, but be careful, because, as the story of little women teaches, everything can suddenly change forcing us, if we have not built a solid and well diversified portfolio, to make many sacrifices. In this regard, it may be useful to know that some currencies and some commodities are considered safe haven assets or financial instruments that can "protect" investments when stock markets fall (as could happen to bonds).

Gold (and precious metals in general), the US dollar and the Swiss franc are the most common ones but it should be understood that their price could also fall, like that of stocks and bonds, even if, with an high probability, this could happen at a different time and therefore help diversify the risks present in the portfolio. They are therefore not a safe heaven in the true sense of the word and one must know they do not guarantee a profit, or a yield forever. Even the gold price can go down and for long periods!

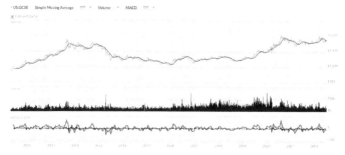

GOLD PRICE

Unfortunately, even gold -and many commodities-like the US dollar and the Swiss franc, while representing precious assets whose availability is undoubtedly limited or strong economies, are subject to the whims of the markets and to what a famous economist called, in the Thirties, the "animal spirits" or the instinct of man for which he sometimes buys and sometimes sells, ignoring these basic rules and following only his emotions. Look in the graphs below, for example, at what happened in the last twenty years to the exchange rate (ie the price expressed in euros) of the US dollar. A continuous ups and downs that saw the euro rise until 2008 and then fall until 2015, when a more lateral movement began to this day, if viewed from far away. In fact, the daily, weekly, monthly variations have been in many cases significant.

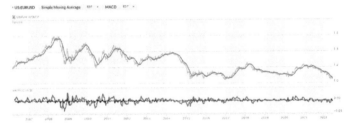

EUR vs USD

We need to bear in mind that even in the case of currencies and commodities the risk of incurring in a loss is not zero and it may be useful to know more before approaching them.

The purchase of a currency presupposes the definition of the price of that currency, expressed in a base currency, or an exchange rate. For example, for us European citizens the base currency is the euro. If we buy US dollars, it is because we think that the price of the US dollar in euro (ie the dollar euro exchange rate) will go up. 2 currencies and the relative supply and demand of the same are always involved. If the demand for dollars is greater than that for euros, the dollar will rise, unless there are significant changes in the supply that act in the opposite direction. If the future supply of dollars is greater than that of the euro, with the same demand, the dollar will fall.

What does the demand and the supply of any currency depend on? The demand depends on the uses of that currency: salaries, payments for the purchase of goods and services, financial transactions (e.g. the purchase of Apple's shares in dollars).

The supply depends on the central banks, which not only physically print banknotes and coins and hold certain currencies as reserves (the US dollar, the euro, the pound sterling, the yen, the Swiss franc and the Chinese yuan), but also control, as we have seen before, monetary policy, or the official interest rates on which all other rates rely (current accounts, mortgages, loans, etc. etc.).

Very easily, if a dollar current account yields more than a euro current account, there could be many people or institutions willing to change their euros into dollars (thus asking for more dollars) and deposit them in the former account denominated in dollars on which they will earn more. In this way, the dollar rises (it appreciates) and the euro falls (it depreciates).

A currency with greater uses then tend to appreciate more because it is more in demand in the real economy. For this reason, the US dollar, used in the exchange of many goods and raw materials, is considered a strong currency, although in the last decades China and Europe have repeatedly tried to overtake it with the euro and the renminbi. It is above all the macroeconomics, therefore, that influences the trend of currencies, as happens for government bonds where politics, central banks and macroeconomic data are the main source of information on which investors decide what they will buy and sell. Unlike shares and bonds issued by companies for which the microeconomics also has its weight.

Currencies are among the most liquid and most traded investments in the world because the Forex market is open 24 hours a day and is huge trillions and trillions (about 5.1, where a trillion is 1 million billion). Unlike the stock markets, it does not have a physical location (it is said to be Over the counter) and trading takes place between Banks electronically day and night.

Unlike currencies, however, commodities are traded on several markets that have become famous for this activity. The best known is perhaps the so called Nymex. Not only gold and silver are raw materials, but also wheat, flour, orange juice or oil, natural gas and many others. The bargaining of these goods takes place through the so called futures, or contracts that establish the delivery in the future of a given quantity paid at today's price.

Investors are not normally interested in buying the physical asset but simply betting on the price trend. For this reason, it is difficult for them to buy gold bars or bags of flour or barrels of oil, of which they wouldn't know what to do with them and where to keep them. They normally buy or sell (depending on whether they expect a price rise or fall) a futures contract and, if the contract is sold before its expiration, this delivery will not be made and the investor will either gain or lose depending on the price movement. Futures are also called derivatives and can have as underlying, other than commodities also currencies, bonds and stocks … i.e. everything!

Their use increased considerably over the years and is not immediate. One thing that distinguishes them and that must be absolutely clear is that they expose you to a very high risk of gain or loss, because they incorporate a so called leverage effect. In fact, to open a futures contract, it is not necessary to have all the money needed to buy the entire amount of commodities, currencies or any of the underlying but a much lower but constant margin is required.

With futures it is possible to do incredible things because the bets can be not only on the rise (if I buy) but also on the fall in prices (if I sell). Futures give ample space to the creativity of finance but require a lot of attention for the reasons just outlined. An instrument similar to futures, in that it is classified as a derivative, is that of options, which do not require you to buy or sell like the former but give you the ability to do so.

Another way to invest while earning when the price of the stock (bond or currency or other) falls is, they say, to be short on that stock which is the opposite of being long.

When we buy stocks, bonds, currencies we have a long position and we earn if the price goes up and we sell.

The financial markets, however, allow us to sell shares, bonds, currencies while not owning them, making it possible to take a short position that will lead to gains if the price falls. In fact, it is possible to borrow them from banks by paying interest. The selling price is today's price, while the borrowed shares will be returned to the bank, buying them back on the market when the investment is closed. In this way, if the price has dropped, the gain will be given by the difference with today's price (higher) taking into account the interest on the loan made by the bank. Selling stocks, bonds, currencies without holding them, or going short, therefore means thinking that the price of that asset will drop because I expect bad micro or macroeconomic news. Like the purchase, it is a risky investment because, if the price will rise and it does not fall because that news do not arrive, the loss will be concrete when closing that short.

The first operation of this type was made in the distant 1600s by a Dutch investor almost by mistake and, since then, at different times, short selling has often been discussed because it gives the opportunity to exasperate the most speculative practices while sometimes neglecting the ethics by which noble finance should always be inspired. Why betting on bad companies and the fall of their price or, even worst, why hoping to see the price of a good company to go down?

In 2008, in the midst of the great financial crisis, or in 2020 during the first pandemic of the global era, it was therefore banned in order to prevent the heavy collapses in prices due to the sale of holders of shares, bonds, currencies, to get back their money was amplified by the speculative sale of those who did not have securities.

7

F AS FAMILY AND FUND

The financial instruments we have explained in the previous pages using the names of the March sisters, can be purchased individually or in "families" that take the name of mutual investment funds.

Mutual funds represent a very disomogeneous universe: there are funds composed only by equities, or only by bonds, by currencies, by commodities and funds that combine and mix several instruments at the same time following a given asset allocation more or less strictly.

In any case both types ensure an high degree of diversification if compared to the purchase of the single stock or bond even if we are buying just one product (a fund) whose composition will be changed an updated by its portfolio manager depending on macro and micro news.

The mutual fund can be bought (subscribed) in banks or on several platforms. It is the same product for all who buy it. It has a daily price that is equivalent to the average of the prices of the instruments it has within it, each in proportion to its weight. You collect the subscriptions, or investments, and in exchange you receive one or more shares whose price (NAV), from that moment, will rise or fall exactly as it happens for a single financial instrument or for an index, determining the gain or the loss (or yield) if you decide to sell it.

The composition of the fund is the hands of a professional other than the financial consultant we have talked about so far who follows, day by day, what happens to each instruments and decide when buy or sell part or all the exiting positions or add new instruments. The portfolio manager works normally in companies called asset management companies, which invest the money raised among the investors by the financial consultant. The portfolio manager sits next to many other professionals who help him to monitor the complexity of markets. They are analysts, economists, strategists. Each of them has a specific role. If analysts monitor individual stocks and bonds (microeconomics), the economist looks at the growth and the inflation of countries (macroeconomics). The strategist is responsible for the so called asset allocation, called also strategy, and according to the moments, based on what is happening, both at a microeconomic and macroeconomic level will advice on the the preferred asset to hold in the portfolio trying to reply to such questions: more equity or more bonds? Gold or silver? Usd or Yen?

Diversification of assets and professionality of the manager do not mean that funds are safe or always profitable. Even professionals can make mistakes. The risk is latent in every investment, and therefore mutual funds as stocks, bonds, currencies and commodities can loose money but it is correct to say that the risk may be lower.

In general, in fact, the diversification of funds reduces risks and many of them have the opportunity to do well on average, or, even if not every day, in the space of a year, three years, five years they can be able to earn.

Funds are divided by groups and for each there is at least an index and a category average. In recent years, the universe of funds has become huge. They can be classified by financial instrument (equity, bonds, currencies, commodities, multi asset), by geographical area (global, US, Europe), by sectors, by theme, by management style, etc. etc. etc.

The distinction between active and passive deserves a mention. The former are funds where the choice of components is at the discretion of the manager while the latter replicate an index or buy its own securities, taking care that they have the same weights as they have in the index. For example, a passive equity fund in the USA could have the same securities as the S&P500 (one of the most common index in USA).

Passive funds have the same trend as indices while active ones can deviate, leading to gains or losses versus the indexes themselves.

Recently many of the mutual funds have begun to focus their attention on the so called social ly responsible investments (SRI), much loved by young people and women, if one think about the sensibility raised by a young Swedish girl, Greta Thunberg, in schools around the world in the last years.

Investing responsibly means investing by rewarding those companies that behave well, not only in respect of the Environment (for example by polluting less), but also of the Society as a whole promoting diversity and the rights of workers and shareholders, assuring a good corporate Governance.

Responsible investing has become very important in recent years and I believe it will continue to attract many investors, to the extent that it will confirm over time that the returns of financial instruments managed with this approach can outweigh those of financial instruments that do not.

Knowing that with our savings and our investments we can contribute to improve the future of the world is very fascinating and helps to give a new dignity to finance, so many times involved in the past in scandals and serious crises causing the rise of skepticism around it.

There are nowadays many SRI funds where the selection of securities is driven by exclusion criteria of certain sectors (for example, companies that produce weapons and cigarettes) or that take environmental impact into account by investing in companies that increase the use of alternative sources of energy or that are committed to reduce their carbon emissions.

In this immense universe of mutual funds (SRI and not), it is not easy to navigate and a careful analysis is needed in order to choose a fund that does not sink, a fund that despite possible moments of not brilliant performances, i.e. negative, on average achieves a positive return.

Morningstar is perhaps the most immediate provide to help in the analysis. Mornigstar is a sort of Michelin guide that gives from 1 to 5 stars to funds, grouped by categories, based on their performance. It is important to know that it is a quantitative analysis in the sense that it uses numbers – for example the returns of the funds in one year, three years, five years and other measures. The stars of a fund as any other ranking could be very useful but cannot be the only analysis. It may be useful to conduct as well a qualitative analysis (on the company, on the team, on the investment process, etc) to complete the information we have before investing.

Although funds, as families of securities, may be less risky than buying a single stock or bond, it may be worth avoiding the Do it Yourself and asking for the advice of a good financial advisor whose contribution is both quantitative and qualitative.

I would be wary of the consultant who offers little choice because, in reality, the options are many and I would suggest to be careful about the costs! It is good to ask about the overall costs from the subscription to the sale of the fund! Each mutual fund may have entry fees, management fees and exit fees. These are the costs incurred to pay all the professionals involved and leave a margin to the asset management company that created and sold the fund. The costs are listed in the documents to read before investing where we find all the information about the profile of risk and return of the fund. In recent years, the competition between asset management companies and the creation of passive funds (characterized by lower costs) has led to a decline in commissions and the trend may not be over, if we consider that digitalization, with the advent of virtual financial advisors could increase competition.

8

JO, THE FUTURE OF FINANCE

In the original Little Women, Jo is a writer and for passion and for money she challenges the common thinking of those years to fulfil her modern and revolutionary dream: to write a book whose sale will give her the money to help her family and allow her to become an independent woman who does not need a good marriage at any cost. A dream potentially revolutionary because able to change the social rules of the time and the life of millions of women.

Finance, like Jo, today could play an active role to change the world thanks to the firepower of money invested in the shares and securities of thousands of companies and governments, while wearing a new dress and assuming a more ethical dimension, containing scandals and fraud and removing the consequent scepticism of many people in investing.

And with courage like Jo, many little women of today will be able to contribute tomorrow to change the world with proper financial education and their investments, helping to correct the distortions that the entire economic system has created in recent decades and still in front of us.

The scandal of Enron, the American energy giant, or that of Volkswagen, one of the largest German car manufacturers, or that of Parmalat, in the milk industry: stories of rigged balance sheets or documents and large financial holes that led to colossal losses by burning millions and millions of savings of small as well as large investors who had bought the stocks and bonds of those companies. Argentine and Greek bonds, overwhelmed by the mismanagement of the public budget of their countries, have not been able to return to all the investors the savings they had invested.

On the one hand, investors must learn to choose virtuous companies and governments, knowing that today there are tools that help in doing this and avoiding being lured by excessive returns, because, as we have remembered in the preceding pages, high returns always correspond to high risks. But on the other hand, companies and governments whose shares and bonds represent the most common investments are pushed today to be more respectful of investors, workers and the environment.

The push comes from the United Nations which in 2015 defined 17 objectives for the planet called Sustainable Development Goals (SDGs), which companies and governments around the world are invited to respect by 2030.

SDGs are very ambitious goals that governments, in collaboration with the companies placed on their lands, are called to pursue in order to create by 2030 a world whose development is sustainable, that means a world where the production of goods and services contributes to the creation of a better planet in which hunger and poverty decrease and the respect for the environment, for gender diversity, for work, for justice increases. A world in which the economy does not prevail over ecology or equality, as has often happened in the recent past.

All of us are called to play our role in everyday life as citizens and as workers (think of waste sorting or complaints of unfair practices against minors or categories at risk).

But what matters most is that even companies and governments will have to behave in a virtuous manner, in order to respect each of those goals. Virtuous will be those companies that demonstrate that they undertake all the possible actions to minimize carbon emissions, respect their employees, encourage diversity, act in compliance with justice by helping to raise the quality of life of the place or places where they are based. And the governments that will allow this to happen will be virtuous by equipping themselves with a set of suitable laws and a judicial system that provides for adequate sanctions in case of violation.

The financial sector has taken up the challenge launched by the United Nations with enthusiasm.

First, many asset management companies are committed themselves to become "better companies"

1) ensuring better working standards for their employees;
2) promoting greater respect for diversity;
3) encouraging a lower environmental impact through, for example, a lower consumption of paper, plastic and making the most of natural sources of energy;
4) respecting its shareholders (even the smallest ones).

At the same time thanks to the purchase of the shares and bonds of many companies belonging to the all the sectors in order to invest their clients' money, the asset managers as shareholders have the opportunity to influence the choices of the invested companies participating at their meetings and voting in favour of behaviours that respect the objectives of the United Nations (this practice is also called engagement).

It is important to believe in it and to insist, as Jo does with her book.

Although with governments it is more difficult, also in this case the inclusion or exclusion by a large investment funds of the securities they issue will increasingly depend on how virtuous they will be, i.e. on how well they will behave towards sustainability respecting Ecological, Social and Governance goals as described by the UN.

ESG is on of the name used to identify the funds we have talked about previously, which include the most virtuous companies and governments in compliance with the 17 objectives of the Nations United. More in general the spectacular growth of the so called sustainable funds between 2010 and 2020 confirms the strong interest of investors. According to Morningstar and TrackInsight at the end of 2020 the sustainable funds were 3087 vs 1304 in 2010.

There is a goal, among the social ones, that is particularly close to my heart and inspired unconsciously Mrs Alcott many years ago while writing her Little Women. It's the fifth, the Gender Parity.

The UN affirms that "gender equality is not only a fundamental human right, but a necessary condition for a prosperous, sustainable and peaceful world." To offer to women and girls equal access to education, health care, decent work, as well as representation in political and economic decision-making processes will give new life to the sustainable economy, bringing large-scale benefits to society and humanity. 143 nations have included the right to equality between men and women in their National Law as early as 2015. But many have remained silent, demonstrating that social and regulatory inequality still prevails in too many nations. Although that of gender equality is a goal in its own right, many other objectives of the 2030 Agenda can only be achieved when the needs of women are considered equal to those of men.

Among the urgent issues to be addressed there are several traditional practices that harm the private sphere, such as female genital mutilation that needs to be stopped and condemned everywhere. According to the World Health Organization 200 milions of girls have undergone the mutilation and every year 3 milions of girls are at risk. In 2022, this is a shame and happens in more than 30 countries, number that could increase with immigrations flows.

Even if the percentage of early marriages -another bad practice against women's rights- has been declining over the past few decades, there is not a single country where this practice has been completely eliminated and potentially reaching the targets set by goal number 5 by 2030. If current trends remain unchanged, between 2017 and 2030 150 million girls will marry before they turn 18. Although the practice of child brides is 4 times more widespread among the poorer social classes than the wealthy ones, it is necessary for nations to accelerate progress in all social groups, in order to eliminate this practice by 2030.

Achieving gender equality requires the introduction of binding regulations aimed at increasing women's emancipation and the irrefutable need for secondary education, including financial, for all girls. The wish of this goal is the disappearance of gender discrimination and the emancipation of women. The importance of "listening to women" has been stressed several times, as a radical change can only be achieved with their active participation. It is their priorities that must determine the priorities of this goal. Women should be seen not only as beneficiaries of the change, but as active players of it. Involving them in building a sustainable and equal world is therefore crucial.

I hope that the institutions will think of solutions that do not deviate from the long and tiring journey already covered up to this point but that, on the contrary, will help women to continue on the path of emancipation of which Jo, Marmee and Louis May Alcott felt the fascinating call many years ago. Today more than ever, in this difficult time post pandemic emergency, women need help from institutions.

Finance can continue to make its contribution not only for the reasons already mentioned when talking about socially responsible investments and ESG factors, but also thanks to a growing female presence in asset management companies and banks. More and more women will invest not only their savings but also those of the community as men have been doing for many years, in respect of the gender parity invoked by the United Nations, which enriches this sector with a different sensibility.

Women and men are different but deserve equal opportunity and their difference is a huge value for the financial sector as well as for every other sector.

Focusing on finance, it is demonstrated statistically that men and women are different both in the management of money – with a different risk aversion, on average lower in women – and in communication skills – men have a leaner style, on average less empathetic, more technical. And scientific studies show how, in communication, men and women activate different parts of the brain. Researchers at the University of Pennsylvania a few years ago underwent magnetic resonance imaging about a thousand people, males and females of various ages, and found that in the male brain the connections run from front to back along the same hemisphere, while in the female the connections are also transverse, from the right hemisphere to the left one, thus facilitating communication. The man, these studies tell us, has a brain that follows patterns based more on rationality, while in the woman the brain functioning is more intuitive and in men the functioning of the nervous circuits is more rigid while it is more flexible in women.

Scientists explain in this way why women are better in multitasking, that is, doing more things together, or more intuitive, why they show more empathy and have better social skills. Men, on the other hand, excel in motor activities, where muscles are used, and are more capable of analysing space, orienting themselves, understanding maps.

Harvard Medical School researchers then found an higher density of neurons in areas of the female temporal cortex connected with linguistic and emotional functions. This means that women are more likely to communicate emotions verbally and express feelings. According to these studies, other particularly developed areas of the female brain are the hippocampus, the main center for controlling emotions and forming memories, and the set of useful circuits for observing the emotions of others. An important difference is also that relating to an area considered the guardian of emotions, called the amygdala due to the shape that makes it resemble an almond. The amygdala is the brain center of fear, anger, aggression, and on average is larger in men than in women.

Also for cultural heritage, women are different from men: biologically designed for creation, for the survival of the human species, for the care of children, women have in fact remained in caves for centuries, taking few risks given the high stakes: the life. All this could explain why women have a high risk aversion and a natural long-term propensity even in the financial space which helps them in investment choices because many of the mistakes in making an investment are caused by impatience and hurry, looking for immediate and huge returns as hungry people seated in front of big cake.

Women investors, women managers or women consultants are in other words different from men and their diversity is something that modern society cannot ignore and take value to a real Modern Society.

My hope is that goal number 5 of the 2030 Agenda will really be achieved and that the little women of the new millennium, properly educated, will have the opportunity to work, earn, save, invest and be independent. And I hope that this will happen soon in any area, not just in finance where, if it is true that a long way has already been done, there is still a lot to do, especially when you move up to roles and responsibilities.

In an effort to understand theory from practice, I finally leave you with the testimonials of some investment experts I have known over the years. They are what L Alcott would call "Jo's friends", known over the years and who play important roles in the companies they work for. They struck me for the passion they put into their work, as well as for their ability to interpret the world through the micro and macro data and news they encounter on a daily basis. I asked them, financial experts in various areas, what they do and when and what their first investment was. But above all, I asked what investment suggestions they would give to our four little women: Amy, Beth, Meg and Jo. After all, like I said at the beginning, each of them is not only the character of the novel but represents, in a timeless and spaceless dimension, the example of a young woman defined by her character and her inclinations in which it is not at all difficult even today mirror.

9

JO'S FRIENDS

Jole Saggese

What is your job?

I am a broadcast journalist and I cover finance and economics. Choosing, probably, "male" topics is part of my nature. Challenging myself in something that doesn't belong to me in order to learn about a topic that fascinates me and at the same time scares me. Kind of like when, as a child, you have to open the checked notebook even though you would have liked the ruled ones. Or when, as you get older, you have an equation and hold your breath until you write the final little number.

Being a woman: a challenge or an opportunity for your work?

Being a woman is a challenge at first that then turns into an opportunity.

At first you are surprised that they are surprised that in addition to being a woman you are also more or less good. Then, the fact that you are a woman and, deemed prepared, becomes a chance you can play.

Do you remember your first investment? How old were you? How long did you hold it?

The fear of losing everything, the abandonment panic has always marked me. And so, I wanted to see and touch my money. What to make? A studio apartment. That's how I started. Only when I sold the studio apartment and bought a bigger house did I realize it was time to think about something else, too. About what? In order not to make rash choices so as not to be influenced by the daily information acquired by following the market, I chose to rely on a professional. A woman, of course. My financial advisor.

What would you advise four young nieces and nephews in the role of a modern Aunt March?

To always go for the money--not the good money but the money that can be made by choosing an investment that puts heart, courage and head together. My profession unfortunately does not allow me to make more detailed suggestions, but I believe that by putting together the courage to take risks, with one's ethical and economic rationality one can make very good investments.

Orazio Di Miscia

What is your job?

I am the head of Asset Allocation and Traditional Investments of the largest insurance companies in Italy. I am in charge of defining the strategic asset allocation ("SAA") and implementing the investment strategy, for the liquid investment component. The task is, therefore, to design the long-term investment strategy taking into account commitments to policy holders, ensuring portfolio diversification and business sustainability for the company also through illiquid investments, of private markets. In the strategy implementation phase, the task is confined to the investment and management of the liquid global asset classes in which the insurance portfolios are invested consistently with the SAA.

Do you remember your first investment? How old were you? How long did you hold it?

The first investments on a personal level were made right after graduation. They were the first investments in stocks but mostly options, trying to leverage and putting to work, and I would say even at risk, the meager financial assets of the time.

What would you recommend for a particularly sensitive woman like Beth?

I imagine for Beth a natural long-term horizon, looking for stability and containment of risk and therefore with a balanced approach between yield and volatility of investments, the ideal portfolio for her could be 30 percent global government bonds, 35 percent good quality corporate bonds, 5 percent high yield corporate bonds, 10 percent emerging market bonds, 15 percent equities and 5 percent gold.

Raffaella Tommaselli

What is your job?

I manage mutual funds, particularly high yield bonds i.e. issued by risky companies with lots of debt.

Being a woman: a challenge or an opportunity for your work?

Being a woman in this job is undeniably (as in any industry) challenging, and being a woman and a mother inevitably involves career sacrifices.

Do you remember your first investment? How old were you? How long did you hold it?

25 years old. My first investment was a 30-year BTP, still in my account.

What would you recommend to a woman who wants to go live abroad like Amy?

I imagine Amy naturally young and with a job. I would suggest that she invest at least 50 percent of her entire portfolio in stocks (including 15 percent in emerging stocks), 20 percent in corporate bonds, 10 percent in alternative investments, and 10 percent in cash to meet unpredictable expenses.

Giordano Beani

What is your job?

I am responsible for multi-asset funds (with stocks, bonds, etc) for an important asset management company.

Do you remember your first investment? How old were you? How long did you hold it?

I think Brioschi shares in 1990 (26 years old). Brioschi was and still is a real estate holding company, I don't even remember why I bought them, but surely back then it was a rumored market and some colleague had given me the "tip of the century," with the result that most of the time I just lost money as it was that time.

What would you recommend to a young single woman like Jo who has some money away?

A young woman with some savings who is unmarried and without children should have at least a 50 percent allocation of her savings in stocks. This is because in the long run, stocks have been shown to earn higher returns than bonds, but one must precisely have a long time horizon without having to use those savings for expenses in the short run. Another way to accumulate equities could be to start with 30 percent, but to make accumulation plans that provide an additional monthly payout so as to smooth out the volatility of the equity markets. The composition of the equity component of the portfolio should favor the U.S. market, which is the largest market and is characterized by the presence of companies at the forefront of technological innovation. Then one could diversify an equity portion into thematic funds such as those related to the aging population, health care, urbanization and "clean" transportation, and "disruptive" innovation, typical of those companies with business models capable of changing and revolutionizing the rules of the game in an industry. If Jo also had a sensitivity to the environment and good corporate practices, so-called SRI funds, i.e., Sustainable and Responsible Investment, could also be included. These funds invest in companies that, in addition to traditional financial parameters, are also distinguished by extra-financial good practices on environmental, social and corporate governance issues (issues called ESG). As for the bond segment, today we are living in a world of low yields, but that the Covid-19 crisis has driven up much of the corporate bond components (corporate bonds). So the allocation of the bond component should favor investments in corporate bonds that are predominantly of high creditworthiness, that is, characterized by a good balance sheet and corporate liquidity. A residual portion can be invested in emerging market bonds, which offer significantly higher yields than Developed countries but are characterized by a higher level of risk. Finally, assuming Jo has an environmental spirit, there are funds that invest in bonds that are called "green bonds" in English. The name comes from the fact that the proceeds from the issuance of these bonds are used by companies to finance investment projects exclusively aimed at protecting and improving the environment.

Viola Benini

What is your job?

I work in a multi family office, that is, in an office that manages money for many families with significant assets, having been a financial advisor following the so-called High Worth Net Individuals, that is, the Bank's "VIP" clients.

Being a woman: a challenge or an opportunity for your work?

At the moment, with grown daughters I would say that the gender factor does not have much weight in my work, however, I spent my previous 20 years within multinational banking structures with a quite competitive environment. When I had little girls it took a lot of willpower and some sacrifice of my private sphere to reconcile everything.

Do you remember your first investment? How old were you? How long did you hold it?

My first financial investment was in the mid-1990s (i.e., more or less 24 years old) in a basket of stocks recommended to me by my bank's advisor and which I sold after a few years and badly (i.e., at a loss) needing money because I had to move to Milan.

What would you recommend to a particularly sensitive woman like Beth?

I think I would suggest to her a defensive portfolio to limit possible swings and losses, made of only 25 percent stocks. For a sensitive woman like Beth I think I would choose mostly socially responsible investments, a lot of cash (at least 15 percent) and corporate bonds and/or funds belonging to strategies decoupled from equity markets for more than 50 percent.

Teodor, Naumov

What is your job?

I manage people's money and people who manage money, meaning I invest the savings of Italians and I am responsible for a team that helps me do that.

Do you remember your first investment? How old were you? How long did you hold it?

"The shoemaker's children walk barefoot" ... and so even I am not a great investor of my own money. However, the first investment was to come and do take my master's degree in Italy. I was 22 years old.

My first financial investment was at the age of 21 when in my country, Bulgaria, privatization of state companies was starting, that is, you could for the first time buy their shares because they were being listed. I invested a small amount of money in 3 companies: a brewery, a sock factory and a tour operator. Of the first two I still have shares today, some 20 years have passed.

What would you recommend to a mom like Meg with three children to secure their future?

The future as a distant one is by definition uncertain. It might be appropriate to invest in different kinds of assets by applying, as I often suggest to my clients, the rule of thirds: one-third stocks, one-third bonds (government and corporate) and one-third commodities, real estate indices and investments that protect against inflation.

Giorgio Castiglioni

What is your job?

I am an investment director and manager of asset management at the bank I work for.

Do you remember your first investment? How old were you? How long did you hold it?

I must have started with Italian government bonds then I switched to equities but I don't remember the age, I just remember that I was already a stock broker, that is, a professional in the field. Then I started investing in futures and options. Since I got into funds, these represent my main investments. Certainly the first investment is no longer in my portfolio!

What would you recommend to a mom like Meg with three children to secure their future?

I would advise her to have a well-diversified portfolio, also built entirely in mutual funds with a fair exposure to stocks, about 40 percent. The rest split between bonds (about another 40 percent) and, for ongoing expenses, a 15 percent extremely liquid investment (bonds with very short maturities). And why not, some gold (5%) to protect against the unexpected.

Francesca Cordella

What is your job?

I deal with personalized portfolios for an important Italian bank.

Being a woman: a challenge or an opportunity for your work?

A challenge because the financial sector still remains male-dominated in decision-making roles. An opportunity because I do a job that I really enjoy and allows me to always have an early look at the future.

Do you remember your first investment? How old were you? How long did you hold it?

I started " ready away" with "do-it-yourself" equity investments in the Italian market in the late mythical 90s . I was about 30 years old. I no longer have those investments partly because some of those companies no longer exist.

What would you recommend to a particularly sensitive woman like Beth?

Beth is a very sensitive, altruistic and music-loving girl. I think today's Beth would prefer to delegate the management of her savings to reduce the impact of emotionality when it comes to investments. I would choose for her the theme of sustainable investments with an equity component (around 30 percent) focused on dividends to be donated in part to the support of young musical talent.

Alessandro Solina

What is your job?

I am investment director.

Do you remember your first investment? How old were you? How long did you hold it?

When I was 24, I bought dollars. I did it through an option (something like futures) that exposed me to an even higher risk of gaining (and losing) because it was leveraged. Unfortunately, it went bad and so instead of the car I should have bought with that money, I ended up with nothing. But there is a moral... Since then I don't particularly like speculative currency investments, which I use only for hedging purposes (in order not to have the exchange rate risk on an investment bought in dollars, for example, I sell dollars for an equal amount but it gets too technical).

What would you recommend to a woman who wants to go live abroad like Amy?

To a woman (like a man...)who wants to go live abroad, I would recommend an absolutely international portfolio made up of 70 percent (40-30) U.S. stocks and bonds. A 25 percent European high-yield and/or convertible bonds and 5 percent emerging dollar bonds. Whether or not to hedge foreign exchange risk might depend on Amy's choice ... if she chose to live in New York I would probably advise against it!

Laura Nateri

What is your job?

I work in the financial sector, for an investment management company. I am responsible for the business development and the coordination of the Italian team.

Being a woman: a challenge or an opportunity for your work?

A fact, not always easy to handle, but one to deal with in order to grow professionally. An opportunity to learn from those who sit in the control room, a challenge because stepping up in a world that speaks a different language requires courage and determination and a not inconsiderable deployment of energy. It is always a chance to put yourself out there, broaden your horizons and become stronger and more confident. It should never be an alibi.

Do you remember your first investment? How old were you? How long did you hold it?

I started working in a bank when I was not yet 24 years old, and after my first salaries I took out a 10-year insurance policy: a form of forced savings -100 euros a month - with a tax benefit that was reimbursed every year as a tax credit. When it expired - 34 years old, a new family, 2 little girls - those little revalued savings were used to finance part of the renovation work on the house I had just bought.

What would you recommend to a mom like Meg with three children to secure their future?

It is necessary to start thinking about the children's future from the first days of their lives. This allows you to have a long enough time horizon to invest in the stock markets, best with an accumulation plan: a form of forced savings, which allows easy planning, is flexible, and generates capital over time that can be liquidated at any time.

Thinking about children's futures also means relieving them of financial commitments and ensuring that they have a basis to continue in case of unforeseen events: life and accident insurance on parents, and covering the mortgage in case of premature death, are useful tools for managing long-term financial planning. Last but not least, teaching them the importance of financial independence and educating them to manage their own financial resources are the foundations to prepare them for a better future.

Kirsty Desson

What is your job?

I am an Investment Manager responsible for managing ~US$2.0bn held in abdrn's Global Smaller Companies funds.

Clients, such as charities, pension funds and wealth management companies, allow us to manage money on their behalf with the aim of growing those assets over time.

My job involves researching and analysing potential new investment ideas and monitoring existing holdings in the funds, as well as reviewing investment ideas put forward by the rest of the team to help build a cohesive stock portfolio taking into account risk parameters within the fund.

The role is enormously rewarding. Having a real purpose in terms of looking after someone's savings, the chance to meet inspirational leaders, to travel and to work in a varied, dynamic, intellectually stimulating environment is rare and special opportunity.

Do you remember your first investment? How old were you? How long did you hold it?

One of my first stock recommendations in 2001 was Siam Cement, one of the leading providers of cement in the Thai market. The cement industry in Thailand had been through a period of consolidation following the Asian Financial Crisis and there was limited new capacity coming on stream due to lack of investment. As a result, the supply side of the market was well controlled whilst demand was recovering as governments invested in infrastructure development and many projects which had stalled during the crisis were finally completed.

The purchase was the first recommendation to my team where I had undertaken all the research myself. We bought the stock across several funds and it outperformed the market significantly. It was an extremely gratifying experience and gave me confidence to continue.

How would you suggest to invest money to a Mum of 3 sons like Meg of Little Women to assure their future income?

When looking where to invest, there are a few useful 'rules of thumb' which all investors can follow.

The first is to find companies which have a clear competitive advantage- this may be a strong brand, a superior technology, more efficient operations. In other words, companies that are differentiated from others in the sector because their offering is in some way better versus peers. Preferably such companies are not reliant on the sales of just one product and those products are available in the market today as opposed to several years in the future. Secondly, companies which are able to invest in their own businesses and sustain growth without requiring additional capital from banks or from equity markets are generally well placed to deliver consistent returns. Indicators to look for include profitability, no or low debt levels and positive free cash generation. Lastly, focus on companies which are able to grow independently of the economic cycle. For medium to long term investors, companies with a management strategy that can deliver returns irrespective of market environment appear attractive.

Anne Richards

What is your job?

I'm CEO of Fidelity International which offers investment solutions and services and retirement expertise to a range of customers globally, from large institutions to individuals. Our Purpose is to work together to build better financial futures and for more than five years, our Women & Money campaign has been championing financial wellbeing among women. We are on a mission to close the gender pension and investment gap between men and women and to build a better and more inclusive world which will help women move towards financial security and equality.

Do you remember your first investment? How old were you? How long did you hold it?

Like many, my first investment was through my company pension which came with my first job out of university. Back then, I didn't pay much attention - each month my employer added to my pension pot and my savings were invested into a 'default' investment fund. Over time, I really came to understand the value of workplace pension schemes and how even small additional contributions can really make a difference over the long term.

What advice would you give to the modern-day March sisters to help them achieve financial independence?

The power of saving small amounts on a regular basis cannot be underestimated. Even small sums invested regularly can build up to a substantial savings pot. You also don't need to be an 'investment expert' to get started.

Successful investors aren't those who regularly 'tinker' with their investments. It's much better to invest regularly in a diversified basket of assets and avoid getting distracted by the daily performance of individual investments. It's time in the market that matters the most.

Campbell Fleming

What is your job?

CEO of AssetCo Plc and Chairman, The Big Exchange

Do you remember your first investment? How old were you? How long did you hold it?

19, I invested in an Oil Company in Australia. For about three months when I sold it to buy a new washing machine for my mother...

How would you suggest to invest money to Jo of Little Women, a young single and visionary woman?

I think Jo should think about long term sustainable equities through thematic ETFs, ESG funds or directly so she can enjoy gains over the long term whilst investing in companies that are doing good for people, the planet or both.

Ana Maria Tuliak

What is your job?

I am a Partner – Executive Recruiter, EMEA at Ludgate Search providing executive search, diversity and inclusion advisory services to the Asset Management and Alternatives industry.

Do you remember your first investment? How old were you? How long did you hold it?

My investment journey started when I purchased a flat in London in 2015. I was 26 at the time and have hit 7 years living in London having grown up in a small coastal town in Croatia. This purchase sparked my interest in this apace and I have taken up a course in property investment in 2017. In 2018, I bought a second investment property outside London purely for cashflow and long term value appreciation purposes. I still hold these two properties as these were intended to be long term investments, however I am now keen to diversify my investments and educate myself on investing in other asset classes. On my investment journey, I've learned that it's important to be liquid in economic downturns not only to ride through those difficult times but also to invest.

How would you suggest to invest money to a modern Beth?

I would advise Beth to always invest with a long term view and retain a good amount of liquidity at all times. Buy in the economic downturns and sell when the economy is on its peak. Be patient and diversify your portfolio over time. Remember it's never too late to start or learn about a new type of investment – meeting yourself where you are and staying open minded is key. Finally, surround yourself with like-minded individuals (particularly female), and perhaps even join a female investment community. Read books about the investment mindset and achieving financial freedom. Stay tuned to new investment trends and economic cycles.

Martin Gilbert

What is your job?

I wear a few hats, I am Chairman of Revolut, a challenger digital bank, Toscafund, a specialist fund manager and AssetCo, a start up asset and wealth management business in the UK. I am also Chairman of The Net Zero Technology Centre in Aberdeen and honorary president of VSA, an Aberdeen social care charity.

Do you remember your first investment? How old were you? How long did you hold it?

I started my asset management career as a UK equities fund manager but quickly established my interest lay more in building businesses than individual stock selection. It was this that led to the creation of Aberdeen Asset Management in 1983, which still manages client money today.

How would you suggest to invest money to Amy of Little Women, a young woman who decides to leave her country to live abroad?

No matter where Amy decides to settle, I would encourage her to focus on time not timing. A sensible approach for Amy might be to make regular investments into equities to be held over the long term. With the increasing focus across the asset management industry on the sustainable needs of people and the planet there are lots of options open to Amy to allow her to invest in products that fit with her beliefs and future financial needs.

CONCLUSIONS AND ACKNOWLEDGMENTS

Writing this short book accompanied me during 2020, the year that the Time would cancel from the calendar due to the pandemic.

I prefer to think that not all bad things come to harm and that, despite the many victims - which in part we could perhaps have and should have avoided by letting ourselves be caught less unprepared - it has taught the world a lot.

In the era of borderless and high-speed globalization, the pandemic reminded us of the fragility of our lives and its difficult balance with the planet.

Spaced out and stuck in our homes, we have also digitized ourselves to keep on working, we have discovered the importance of the state and its centrality in front of health and education and several times we talked about resiliency, a word until a few years ago known only by psychologists.

However, Covid19 has triggered a deep economic crisis causing unemployment, especially among women and for the luckier who did not lose their jobs, the closure of schools meant very difficult months of hard reconciliation between work and family life.

I hope that the shortcomings highlighted by the pandemic will be solved so that many more women will be able to access the job market because schools, hospitals and environment, all to be reinforced according to the national plans following the pandemic, require professions with "high femininity". Women have a natural predisposition to take care of the other by themselves and it does not matter whether it is an individual or the planet as a whole.

The female emancipation dear to Marmee, Jo and their fantastic author, May Louise Alcott, will not stop with the pandemic, on the contrary the future and the savings will become more and more "pink" and this will be even more intense if more women will approach professions traditionally with a more masculine vocation and also destined to have more and more importance in the years to come (I am thinking, for example, of technology).

I thank Paola for her brilliant preface and Martin, Jole, Orazio, Raffaella, Giordano ,Viola, Teodor, Giorgio, Francesca, Alessandro, Laura, Anne, Campbell, Kirsty and Ana for their interesting contributions that will probably drive the young readers of this guide in their first investment.

Thanks as well to Giorgia (beautician), Alessia (dancer) and Allegra (graphics) for having posed for the cover.

Finally, a special thanks to my parents for all.